HILARIOUS JOKES FOR MINECRAFTERS

MOBS, CREEPERS, SKELETONS, AND MORE

MICHELE C. HOLLOW, JORDON P. HOLLOW, AND STEVEN M. HOLLOW

Illustrations by Amanda Brack

Sky Pony Press
New York

Copyright © 2016 by Hollan Publishing, Inc.

Minecraft ® is a registered trademark of Notch Development AB

The Minecraft game is copyright © Mojang AB

Sky Pony Press books may be purchased in bulk at special discounts for sales promotion, corporate gifts, fund-raising, or educational purposes. Special editions can also be created to specifications. For details, contact the Special Sales Department, Sky Pony Press, 307 West 36th Street, 11th Floor, New York, NY 10018 or info@skyhorsepublishing.com.

Sky Pony® is a registered trademark of Skyhorse Publishing, Inc.®, a Delaware corporation.

Minecraft ® is a registered trademark of Notch Development AB
The Minecraft game is copyright © Mojang AB

Visit our website at www.skyponypress.com.

10 9 8 7 6 5 4 3 2 1

Library of Congress Cataloging-in-Publication Data is available on file.

Cover design by Brian Peterson
Cover illustration credit Hollan Publishing, Inc.
Cover and interior illustrations by Amanda Brack

Print ISBN: 978-1-5107-0632-3
Ebook ISBN: 978-1-5107-0636-1

Printed in Canada

CONTENTS

Introduction   *iv*

1. Hostile Mobs   1

2. Nether Mobs   31

3. Guardians and Villagers   47

4. Passive and Tamable Mobs   59

5. Snow and Iron Golems   87

6. Steve and Alex   102

7. Herobrine   128

8. Weapons, Flowers, and Jewels   139

9. Orespawn, Mutant Creatures,
       and Twilight Forest Mods   151

10. Minecraft Players   162

Author Bios   172

INTRODUCTION

A joke book about Minecraft can be called niche (or very specific) humor. We, however, are calling it *Notch* humor. If you know Minecraft, you may have groaned or giggled, and you certainly will get that joke. We have found a secret language of sorts that is just shared by you—the fans of the game.

Kids in the gaming world call Minecraft a phenomenon. Your parents may call it an obsession. Fans—you know who you are—keep on coming back because Minecraft nurtures your creativity. It makes perfect sense to compare it to time spent playing in a sandbox or maybe even the original LEGO bricks—the ones before the kits, when nothing held you back. Markus Persson, the creator of the game, once said the only limit in Minecraft is your imagination.

In addition to letting your imagination run wild, Minecraft allows you and your fellow players share a sense of humor. While blowing things up, causing fires, and other forms of destruction may sound ominous in most situations, in Minecraft, these things are sheer fun.

So, in between running from and fighting hostile mobs and trading with villagers, enjoy these jokes, riddles, puns, limericks, poems, tongue twisters, haikus, and trivia facts about your favorite game.

CHAPTER 1

HOSTILE MOBS

JOKES

Q: What happens when a creeper walks into a bar?
A: Everyone dies.

■

Q: Did you hear that the creeper was the life of the party?
A: He had a blast.

■

Q: What popular TV show do ghasts like to watch?
A: *Mobern Family*!

■

Q: Why can Minecraft spiders swim?
A: Because they have webbed feet!

Q: What do you get when you cross an Enderman with a creeper?

A: A teleporting bomb.

Q: What do Minecraft skeletons say before they sit down to dine?

A: "Bone appetite!"

■

Q: Why didn't the skeleton dance at the villagers' ball?

A: He had no body to dance with.

■

Q: How did Steve know that the skeleton was lying to him?

A: He could see right through him.

Q: What song does a blaze like to dance to?
A: "We Didn't Start the Fire."

■

Q: How do hostile mobs start a fairy tale?
A: "Once upon a slime . . ."

■

When I saw the witch with a potion, I knew trouble was brewing.

■

The Wither was confused and didn't know wither he should go to the Nether or not.

■

First zombie to a second zombie: "I'd tell you a joke about the end, but it will just dragon."

■

Q: Why did the creeper cross the road?
A: To escape the ocelot.

■

Q: Why did the Enderman stop playing?
A: Because he was at the end of his game.

Q: Why are there no posters of Endermen in Minecraft?
A: Because no one can look at them.

■

Q: How did the witch kill the player?
A: Her potions just blew him away.

■

Q: Why are Minecraft spiders always angry?
A: Because they keep going up the wall!

■

Q: What did the player say to the slime that he hadn't seen in a while?
A: "You gruesome."

■

Q: Why did the zombie cross the road?
A: To get to the next village.

■

Q: What do mosquitoes and zombies have in common?
A: They like a bite before bedtime!

Q: What kind of parties do creepers have?
A: Block parties.

■

Q: Why can't Endermen read an entire book?
A: Because they always start at the end.

■

Q: What games do zombies play with ants?
A: Squash.

■

Q: What do you say when you meet a Wither?
A: "Bye, Bye, Bye."

■

Q: What's a creeper's favorite toy?
A: A BOOM-a-rang.

■

Q: What do annoyed skeletons call noobs?
A: Blockheads.

Q: What's black and white and rolls off a pier?

A: An Enderman and a chicken fighting over a piece of cooked pork!

■

Q: Why do players shop at Endermen yard sales?

A: To get their stuff back.

■

Q: Why did the Enderman cross the road?

A: He didn't—he teleported.

■

Q: Where does an Enderman sleep?

A: Anywhere he wants.

■

Q: What did the zombie say to his friend who was up playing Minecraft all night?

A: "You look dead tired."

■

Q: What did the creeper call his tired silverfish?

A: A sleepy creepy!

Q: What goes "snap, crackle, pop"?
A: Silverfish in lava.

■

Q: What did one slime say to the other who hit him over the head?
A: "I'll get you next slime!"

Q: What did the zombie say to the new player?
A: "Pleased to eat you."

■

Q: Why did the slime stay home?
A: He had no place to goo!

Q: Why did the silverfish ground his children?
A: Because they were bugging him!

■

Q: Why did the zombie knit an extra sweater?
A: Because he wanted to keep his new family member warm.

■

Q: What did the creeper say to the player?
A: "Open the door, or I'll open the wall!"

■

Q: What do you get when you cross a chicken with a creeper?
A: The Grim Peeper.

■

Q: Why was the zombie happy to be in night court?
A: He was hoping the judge would grant him a new life sentence.

■

Q: What did the zombie say to his date?
A: "I've been dying to meet you."

Q: What do you get when a witch flies a plane?

A: A horror-flying experience.

■

Q: What do you call diamonds given to a creeper in exchange for a favor?

A: A monster bribe.

■

Q: What mobs slow down computers?

A: Rendermen!

■

Q: What's creepy and leads to the second floor of a creeper's house?

A: Monstairs.

■

Q: Where do zombies go hiking?

A: Death Valley.

■

Q: How do creepers like their eggs?

A: Terror fried.

Q: Why did the police hold the creeper after he was hit by lightning?

A: Because the creeper was charged!

■

Q: Why did the zombie leave the restaurant?

A: Because they weren't serving human beans, pickled kids, or eyes scream.

■

Q: Why did the zombie cross the road?

A: To get to the graveyard.

■

Q: Who are the heaviest creatures in Minecraft?

A: Skele-tons!

■

Q: Why does the zombie like ice cream?

A: Because while he's eating you, you scream.

■

Q: Why are creepers tired at the end of the day?

A: Because being evil is hard work.

Q: What type of contests do Endermen hate?
A: Staring contests!

■

Q: What did the mutant creeper say to the mutant Enderman?
A: "Stop sucking me in."

■

Did you know that Endermen scare people out of their mines?

■

Q: Why did the Enderman leave the party?
A: He felt uncomfortable with everyone staring at him.

■

Q: What did the creeper say to the noob?
A: "We hope you enjoy your ssstay."

■

The creeper is always greener on the other side.

■

Q: How many creepers does it take to blow up a lightbulb?
A: Just one! *Kaboom!*

Knock, knock.
Who's there?
Interrupting creeper.
Interrupting creep—
BOOM!

■

Q: What did the mom Enderman say to her child while he was getting dressed?
A: "Don't forget to wear clean *Enderwear*."

■

Q: What did the pig say to the creeper?
A: Nothing. The creeper blew up the pig.

■

Q: What do you call a blown-up creeper?
A: Dead.

■

Q: Why didn't the skeleton cross the road?
A: He didn't have enough guts.

Q: How do zombies and skeletons keep from burning during the day?
A: They stand on soul sand.

■

Q: How is a skeleton like a zombie?
A: They both spawn in darkness and burn in sunlight.

■

Knock, knock.
Who's there?
Creeper.
Creeper who?
Boom!

■

Two creepers walked into a bar. It took months to rebuild.

■

Q: How do you make a creeper destroy himself?
A: Give him a mirror.

First player: "I found a skeleton with a gold medal around his neck."
Second player: "What was on the medal?"
First player: "Minecraft Hide and Seek Champion 2009."

■

Q: Where do zombies like to hang out?
A: In the dead zone!

■

Q: Why was the zombie mad?
A: Because he couldn't get good TV reception when *The Walking Dead* was on!

■

If a creeper blows up in a forest and there is no one there to hear it, did he really make a boom?

If a creeper blows up in the forest and no one is there to see it, does anyone care?

■

Q: What did one creeper say to another other who kept on changing directions?
A: "Make up your mine!"

■

Q: What did the creeper say to the volcano?
A: "I lava you."

■

Q: What did the witch get by mixing a potion of spiders and rabbits?
A: Bugs Bunnies.

■

Q: What did the player say when he saw the creeper?
A: "Here comes the—*BOOM!*"

■

Q: What did the player say when he saw the creeper?
A: "Oh, BLAST!"

Q: **What did the young creeper say to his parents before the party?**
A: "This is going to be a BLAST!"

■

Q: **Why did the witch couple get divorced?**
A: They were driving each other batty.

■

Q: **What did the young zombie say to his parents when he broke the vase?**
A: "Oh, I'm so undead!"

■

Q: **What do you call an Enderman on a diet?**
A: A slenderman.

■

Q: **Why is the creeper so awesome?**
A: Because he blew my mind.

■

Q: **What do you call a skeleton in an ice biome?**
A: A numbskull.

Q: Why did the zombie run away from the player?
A: Because he was playing with fire.

■

Q: What do you call a group of zombies?
A: Mobsters.

■

Q: Two Minecraft zombies were fighting. Which one came out alive?
A: Neither. They're both dead.

■

Q: What did the zombie say when she broke up with her zombie boyfriend?
A: "You're dead to me."

■

Q: What does a vegan Minecraft zombie eat?
A: Raw potatoes, mushrooms, and grains.

■

Q: What is a zombie's favorite TV show?
A: *The Walking Dead.*

Q: What did the noob say to the zombie?
A: Nothing. The zombie killed the noob.

■

Q: What is a skeleton's favorite song?
A: "Can't Torch This!"

■

Q: What do Endermen hate more than being stared at?
A: Mirrors.

■

Q: What do you call an Enderman who spends all of his time at the gym?
A: A pumped up slenderman!

■

Q: Who went into a witch's hut and came out alive?
A: The witch.

■

Q: What goes "cackle, cackle, boom"?
A: A witch who mixes TNT with a bad potion.

Q: **Why wasn't it a big deal when the zombie blew up his own stove?**

A: Because zombies prefer raw food.

■

Q: **What do you get if you cross a witch with a snow block?**

A: A cold spell.

■

Q: **What's the difference between a musician and a zombie?**

A: One composes and the other decomposes.

■

Q: **Why did the skeleton stay indoors on the sunny day?**

A: He wanted to avoid sunburn.

■

Q: **How do you make a creeper smile?**

A: Turn him upside down.

■

Q: **What did the zombie say to the Minecraft player?**

A: "I love you for your brains."

Q: What did the zombie mob say to the noob?
A: "We're dying to have you for dinner."

■

Q: What do zombies say to Minecraft players?
A: "We're dying to meet you."

■

Q: Where do zombies go on vacation?
A: The Dead Sea.

■

Q: Where did the zombie build his house?
A: On a dead-end street.

■

Q: What part of your house do zombies avoid?
A: Your living room.

■

Q: What did the zombie ask the new player?
A: "You want a piece of me?"

Q: Where do zombies like to go swimming?
A: The Dead Sea.

■

Q: What is a zombie's favorite meal?
A: A Steve-wich.

■

Q: What did the zombie say to the player?
A: "You're on tonight's menu."

■

Q: How did you know that the zombie was sleepy?
A: He was dead on his feet.

■

First player: "Eww, there's a small slime in my apple."
Second player: "Hold on, I can get you a bigger one!"

Q: Why did the zombie cross the road?
A: To eat you.

■

First zombie: "How did you become a zombie?"
Second zombie: "It took *dead*ication."

■

Q: How nice was the zombie to the new player?
A: Very—he kept buttering her up.

■

Q: What did the zombie say when the player dug way, way down?
A: "It's mine, mine."

■

Q: Why did the Minecraft player keep on calling the skeleton "Napoleon"?
A: Because he was determined to make him Bone-a-part.

■

Q: What happened to the creeper when he failed to sneak up on a player?
A: He blew his chance!

Q: What kind of crackers do creepers like?
A: Firecrackers!

■

Q: How many zombies does it take to change a torch?
A: None. Zombies prefer darkness.

■

Q: Why did the player get mad at the creeper?
A: Because the creeper was trying to blow him up even
though the player was just mining his own business.

■

The creeper got a job at an explosives factory. The next day,
he got fired.

■

Q: What did the witch say when her potion exploded?
A: "I guess the whole thing blew up in my face."

■

Two zombies are eating a clown and one says to the other,
"Does this taste funny to you?"

Two zombies were sitting at the dinner table when one turned to the other and said, "I hate eating Steve." The other replied, "So try the raw potatoes."

■

Q: What kind of food do zombies refuse to eat?
A: Lifesavers.

■

Q: Why didn't the dog come when Steve called?
A: Because the zombie bit his legs off.

■

Q: In addition to blocks, how do zombies keep others out of their houses?
A: They install dead bolts.

■

Q: Do zombies eat popcorn with their fingers?
A: No, they eat their fingers separately.

■

Q: What's a zombie's favorite bean?
A: A human bean.

Q: Why did the zombie with one hand cross the road?

A: To get to the second-hand shop!

■

Q: Why did the zombie wait to eat the creeper?

A: He had to wait for the green creeper to ripen.

■

Q: Why are Withers forgetful?

A: Because it goes in one ear and out the other.

■

Q: Why do Withers easily forget things?

A: Because everything goes in one head and not in the other two.

■

Q: Which mobs serve the best drinks in Minecraft?

A: Bartendermen!

■

Q: How did the creeper plant the roses?

A: He blew them up.

TONGUE TWISTERS

Which Witch Won With Which Weapon?

Charged Creepers Carry Crafty Crazy Combustible Explosions.

Creepers Chase Courageous Kids.

Which Witch Was Wicked?

Charged Creepers Colliding Cause Creepers to Crumble!

A Skeleton's Sword Slays Skeletons!

Black Back Bats.

Black Batty Bats.

MINECRAFT LIMERICKS, POEMS, AND HAIKUS

Nighttime in Minecraft has come.
The footsteps of zombies would drum.
They marched through the street,
Looking for something to eat.
Take care, or your life will succumb.

As I mined all night long, I went deeper.
I wouldn't stop and dug steeper.
Without sleep I felt brave
And entered a dark cave
And laughed in the face of a creeper.

■

I built a grand villa of rocks.
I used stone and obsidian blocks.
It stands thirty blocks tall.
Creepers try to climb the wall.
Frustrated, they pickaxe the locks.

■

I tried to give the zombie mushroom stew.
He shouted that stew wouldn't do.
"I'm vegan," I told him. "I don't eat meat."
He said he would start with my feet.
So out of the cave I flew.

■

I mine all night
With creepers who come out to fight.
I blow them up with TNT.
Goodness, this game is so much fun for me!

■

When zombies come out at night
They give us a scare and a big fright.
They wander biomes
And love to roam.
If you see one, run with all your might.

■

A zombie ate chickens undead.
And this is what he said:
"It clucked in my belly,
While I watched the telly,
And it clucked as I lay in my bed."

■

I spot a creeper.
He's in need of a big hug.
Closer he comes—BOOM!

■

We call them undead for a reason.
They've committed acts of treason.
Try to chop off their heads.
Watch out if they bled.
In Minecraft, it's zombie-hunting season.

■

There once was a creeper with a big frown.
A player tried in vain to turn it upside down.
When he came near,
The creeper showed no fear.
He blew up the player's town.

■

The player wasn't a leaper.
Instead he dug his pickaxe deeper.
He gave it a go,
And what do you know?
He landed on top of a creeper.

■

Creepers inspire
feelings of utter terror.
Run away quickly.

■

There once was a zombie named Zane.
He was incredibly insane.
His victim—a player—
Failed at defeating this slayer.
Now Zane is enjoying his brains!

■

The safest hideout is in a mall
That I built with locked doors and a thick wall.
Well, now I'm surrounded
And constantly hounded
By a zombie who won't take a fall.

■

There once was a zombie named Ed.
He certainly was quite undead.
He surprised me so
And bit off my toe.
I limp around now filled with dread.

DID YOU KNOW...?

Did you know that a skeleton will shoot itself if you are under or over it?

Did you know that zombies and skeletons won't burn during the day if they are standing on soul sand?

Did you know that creepers have four legs?

Did you know that Endermen have purple eyes?

Did you know that an Enderman's weakness is water?

Did you know that when you summon a Wither it will gain health, explode, and destroy everything?

CHAPTER 2

NETHER MOBS

JOKES

Q: Why don't blazes make good managers?
A: They keep firing people.

■

Q: What did the blaze get when he threw fire at a box of apples?
A: Baked apples.

■

Q: Why is Belgium filled with lava?
A: Because it is next to the Nether-lands.

■

Q: What did the blaze champion say to his opponent?
A: "I won fair and square."

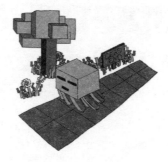

Q: What type of streets do ghasts haunt?
A: Dead ends!

■

Q: Where do ghasts go on holiday?
A: The Nether-lands.

■

Q: Why can't blazes keep their jobs?
A: Because they are always getting fired.

■

Q: Why do ghasts shoot fireballs and not water?
A: Water evaporates.

Q: Why didn't the boat crash?
A: Because it landed on soul sand.

■

Q: What did the ghast say to the player in the Nether?
A: "You're *Nether* going to get out of here!"

■

Q: What did one slime say to the other slime?
A: "Do you mind if I stick with you?"

■

Q: What did one slime say to the other slime when he was leaving?
A: "Slime you later."

■

Q: What did the slime say when he quickly fell off a cliff?
A: "See how fast slime flies!"

■

Q: What do you get when you cross a pig with a blaze?
A: Pork chops.

Q: What do you get when you build a frame out of obsidian and light it with fire?

A: A Nether portal.

■

Q: What did the ghast say when he was stuck?

A: I will *Nether* get out of here.

■

Q: What animals do ghasts sound like?

A: High-pitched cats.

■

Q: What sounds closer than it actually is?

A: A ghast when it is destroying things.

■

Q: What is a ghast's favorite song?

A: "Great Balls of Fire."

■

Q: What's a ghast's favorite food?

A: Pumpkin pie with I-scream.

First player: "Who's the greatest Cubist of the twenty-first century?"
Second player: "Notch!"

■

Q: What did the ghast say when the zombie pigman started showing off?
A: "What a ham."

■

Q: Where does a baby ghast go when his parents are at work?
A: Dayscare.

■

Q: How did the player avoid being attacked by the zombie pigman?
A: He ignored him and *Nether* gave him a thought.

Q: Why did the zombie pigman cross the road?
A: Because he was riding a chicken.

■

Q: How did Peter Pan wind up in the Nether?
A: He took a wrong turn flying to Neverland!

■

Q: How do you get to a ghast's house?
A: Walk down the street until you reach the dead end.

■

Q: What does a ghast say when he's happy?
A: "I'm having a blast!"

■

Q: What does a ghast say when he's upset?
A: "How ghastly!"

■

Q: What did the grandfather ghast say to his grandson who he hadn't seen for a long time?
A: "Wow, you gruesome."

Q: Why was the ghast crying?
A: Everyone he liked blew up!

■

Q: What did the critic say about the ghast's artwork?
A: "It's a monsterpiece."

■

The bookstore owner said to a Wither, "Here's a good book to help you get ahead." The Wither answered, "No, thank you, I already have three heads!"

■

Q: What happened to the snow golem who entered the Nether?
A: He became a puddle.

Q: What's the best way to speak to a ghast?
A: Long distance.

■

Q: Why are ghasts so miserable?
A: Because they find everything ghastly.

■

Q: What type of horses do ghasts ride?
A: Night mares.

■

Q: What is the national anthem of the Nether?
A: "Burn, Baby, Burn!"

■

Q: How did the players in the Nether feel the first time they saw the noob?
A: They were *a*-ghast.

■

Q: Why was the Minecraft player confused?
A: There were two shovels in a chest and he couldn't choose!

Q: Why did the noob leave the mines?
A: He was scared to death of the Nethers.

■

Q: Why are there no cars in Minecraft?
A: Because hostile mobs blocked all of the roads.

■

Q: Why did the bartender throw the baby ghast out of the bar?
A: Because he was a miner.

■

Q: How does a snake scare a ghast?
A: He yells, "Boa!"

■

Q: How did the player feel about the Nether portal?
A: It left him *a*-ghast.

■

Q: What's a blaze's favorite song?
A: "I'm on Fire."

Q: **What song did the blaze like?**
A: "Don't Play with Fire!"

■

Q: **What song did the blaze mob play at the concert?**
A: "Light My Fire."

■

Q: **What dance song was the blaze dancing to?**
A: "Jump into the Fire."

■

Q: **What did the blaze say to the one he loves?**
A: "I'm burnin' for you."

■

Q: **How are slimes like rabbits?**
A: They both hop.

■

Q: **How did the Wither know that the three-headed monster was going to storm into the Nether?**
A: He checked the *Wither* Channel.

Q: What can the smartest Minecraft players solve?
A: Rubik's Magma Cubes!

■

Q: What's a larger, scarier version of a skeleton?
A: A wither skeleton!

■

Q: What did the player do with the Nether wart?
A: He planted it, let it bloom, and used it for brewing potions.

■

Q: How did the player move long distances so quickly?
A: He used a portal in the Nether.

■

Q: How could you tell the zombie pigmen were tired?
A: They were dead on their feet.

TONGUE TWISTERS

Gargantuan Ghastly Ghasts Gather.

Nexus or Nether? Notch Knows.

Players Pass Purple Portals.

Firing Fiery Flaming Fireballs.

Nether Mind Nether Mobs for Nether Mobs don't Mind Miners.

Slimes Spawn in Swamps.

MINECRAFT LIMERICKS, POEMS, AND HAIKUS

Trying to get sleep?
Stay out of the bed, or else
Players will explode!

■

In the Nether you must beware!
Listen to this warning and take care!
Players stay out of beds.
For explosions will shatter your heads!

■

To get a blaze rod
Watch for hurling fireballs.
That the blaze will throw.

■

Duck, quick, be careful.
The blaze hurls large fireballs
Right at you, *kaboom!*

■

Ghasts drop gunpowder
Collect ghast tears when they die
Use them in potions

■

Make ghast-proof buildings.
Use stone from the Overworld.
Ha-ha! You've tricked them.

■

Should you be so bold
to let ghasts fire at you?
They light your portal.

■

Time spent playing Minecraft
is anything but daft.
The possibilities broaden my scope
and fill me with lots of hope.
We insiders get the last laugh!

■

To me, Minecraft is more than a game.
To my parents, my obsession's quite insane.
Blowing up a ghast in the Nether.
Makes me feel better.
Anticipating my next move.
I am in the building groove.

■

The Withers shoot skulls
That look just like their own heads.
Watch out—they explode.

■

If you kill one and collect his head,
Hold on—it's code red.
More are on the rise.
A wither skeleton has hit you by surprise.
Your body withers, and now you're dead.

■

A mixed-up ghast named Jean
Was incredibly wicked and mean.
He chased me around,
And I fell on the ground.
Now Jean got hold of my spleen!

DID YOU KNOW...?

Did you know that there is no way to place water in the Nether? Even smashed or melted ice will not turn into water!

Did you know that you can avoid being hit by a ghast by blocking his line of sight with transparent blocks?

Did you know that killing magma cubes cause them to break and divide?

Did you know that skeletons have cousins in the Nether called wither skeletons?

Did you know that the Wither boss will kill any mob?

Did you know that the wither skeleton can poison you with a potion effect that leeches life away when it hits you?

Did you know that magma cubes are a cousin of Overworld slimes?

Did you know that if you attack just one zombie pigman, all zombie pigmen will also attack?

Did you know that zombie pigmen only spawn in the Nether?

Did you know that zombie pigmen keep on attacking even if you are dead?

CHAPTER 3

GUARDIANS AND VILLAGERS

JOKES

Elder guardian: "What's the main difference between LEGO and Minecraft?"
Ocean guardian: "With LEGO, you don't die."

■

Q: What can be heard up to 100 blocks away?
A: A guardian's laser sound.

■

Q: What happens when blocks break in the ocean?
A: They get wet!

Q: What type of guardian sits on the bottom of the ocean and shakes?

A: A nervous wreck.

■

Q. When elder guardians look back on life, what do they miss the most?

A. Blowing things up!

■

Q: Why did the elder guardian feel ill?

A: His nose was blocked up.

Q: What did the villager say to the other villager?
A: Nothing, because villagers don't talk.

■

Q: What's another name for a villager's hut?
A: A panic room.

■

Q: Which zombie villager won the battle?
A: It was a dead-tie!

■

Q: What did the villagers get when they divided the circumference of a pumpkin by its diameter?
A: Pumpkin pi!

■

Q: Why did the villager fail math?
A: He had a mental block.

■

Q: How did one villager inspire the new Minecraft player?
A: He told him that the world is his Minecraft and he can build anything!

Q: Why did the villagers hold the iron golem over a fire pit?
A: To get the wrinkles out of their clothing.

■

Q: Why are villagers antisocial?
A: They keep saying "Mine, mine, mine."

■

Q: What song do villagers like to hum?
A: "We Built This City."

■

Q: What's a villager's favorite show tune?
A: "It's a Hard-block Life."

■

Q: What did the villagers sing when the Endermen cornered them?
A: "Trapped."

■

Q: Why did the player get a stomachache?
A: He ate too much creepy pasta!

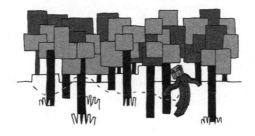

Q: How do crazy villagers go through the forest?
A: They take the psychopath!

■

First villager: "What do you call small slime?"
Second villager: "Slim!"

■

Q: What did the villager-turned-DJ do at the party?
A: He turned the music up a Notch.

■

Q: What did one villager say to the other?
A: "A-u, give me back my gold!"

■

Q: How do creepers play music?
A: On their BOOM boxes.

Q: How can you tell if a villager is in love?
A: He walks very slowly.

■

Q: Why did the zombie villager turn purple and get nauseous for ten seconds?
A: He was cured!

■

Q: Why couldn't anyone tell the two zombie villagers apart?
A: They were dead-ringers!

■

Q: Why did the zombie villager go crazy?
A: Because he lost his mind!

■

First villager: "How many Minecraft players does it take to screw in a lightbulb?"
Second villager: "None. Players use torches."

■

Q: Why was the eighth villager crying on his birthday?
A: Because he had seven guests at his party and it takes seven bites to eat a cake!

Q: Why did the villagers think the skeleton wouldn't attack them?

A: Because the skeleton didn't have any guts.

■

Q: What did one hippie villager say to the other hippie villager?

A: "Hey, man, can you dig it?"

■

Q: What did one villager say to his friend when another villager was rude?

A: "Nether mind him."

■

Q: Why do hip villagers hate Minecraft?

A: Because it's full of squares!

■

First villager: "How do you know when your friends are playing too much Minecraft?"

Second villager: "Just shout 'creeper' and watch everyone dive under their desks."

Q: What has a dog's head and a kitten's tail?

A: A zombie villager coming out of a pet store.

■

Q: Why was the zombie villager off his game?

A: Because he was dead tired!

■

Q: What food would you never see a zombie villager eating?

A: Lifesavers!

■

Q: What room should you build to keep out zombie villagers?

A: A living room!

TONGUE TWISTERS

Billy Bob Built Buildings by Breaking Boulders.

Great Green Guardians Growl.

Groups of Guardians Guard Gracefully.

Elders Eyes Emit Eerie Effects.

Guardians Guarding Gilttery Gold.

Prized Pretty Prismarine.

Trade Trinkets Trade Tools.

Surly Swarms Stinging Strongly.

Minding Manners Matter Most in the Mines.

MINECRAFT LIMERICKS, POEMS, AND HAIKUS

Guardians attack
By sending out laser beams.
Careful, they can kill.

■

Guardians target
And harm players in water.
Avoid the water.

Guardians swim well
Searching for players and squid.
Boats won't keep you safe.

■

Falling to their death.
It takes thirty-two long blocks.
Guardian goes splat.

■

Elder guardians
Spawn in ocean monuments
And are hostile mobs.

■

Elder guardians
Attack firing lasers
And cause mine fatigue.

■

Beware of Elders.
These guardians cause much pain
With thorn-like attacks.

■

Elder guardians
Will drop prismarine crystals
If raw fish drop fails.

■

Elder guardians
Are sometimes spawned through commands
And don't have spawn eggs.

■

I play Minecraft all day and all night.
It gives the villagers a bit of a fright.
They worry that the only sunlight I see
Is the one in the biome with me.

■

Don't leave, villager.
Leaving means you won't return.
You'll be greatly missed.

■

No x-ray vision.
Invisible? We see you!
So don't try to hide.

■

An invisibility potion won't protect.
From guardians it has no effect.
They hope that their ink
Will cause them to sink.
But guardians use their powers to detect.

DID YOU KNOW...?

Did you know that villager children like to play tag?

Did you know that creepy pasta are internet scary stories told in forums and other sites?

Did you know that villagers were once called testificates and that they are intelligent and passive?

Did you know you can cure zombie villagers if you throw a splash potion on them and feed them golden apples?

Did you know that villagers resemble a cavemen Squidward?

Did you know that 5 percent of all zombies are zombie villagers?

Did you know that zombie villagers behave just like ordinary zombies except their heads and face look like villagers with a darker green color?

CHAPTER 4

PASSIVE AND TAMABLE MOBS

JOKES

Q: What happened to the sheep that stepped on a flower?
A: It dyed.

■

Q: Why did the chicken cross the web?
A: To get to the other site.

■

Q: What did one cow say to the other in the tiny hut?
A: "There isn't *mush*room in here!"

■

Q: What happened to the sheep named Jeb?
A: Its wool faded between all the sheep colors.

Q: **What do you get when you cross a cow with a mushroom?**

A: A mooshroom.

Knock, knock.
Who's there?
Interrupting mooshroom.
Interrupting m—
Moooo!

Q: **Did you hear about the cow that tried to escape over a barbed wire fence?**

A: Yes! It was an udder disaster.

Q: What did the cow say to the angry mob?
A: "Moo!"

■

Q: What happened when a large herd of cows was destroyed?
A: It was udder annihilation.

First player: "What a cute bunch of cows on that farm."
Second player: "It's a herd."
First player: "Heard of what?"
Second player: "Herd of cows."
First player: "Of course, I've heard of cows!"

■

Q: Why was the cow broke?
A: Because the players milked it dry.

■

Q: Did you hear about the kitten that ate the sheep?
A: She had mittens!

Q: What do you get when you cross a chicken with a male kitten?

A: A peeping tom.

■

Q: Why is it so hard for ocelots to hide in Minecraft?

A: Because they are always spotted.

■

Q: Why did the cow cross the road?

A: To get to the udder side.

■

Q: Why are some Minecraft cows musical?

A: They make a sound like a kazoo!

■

Q: How do wolves eat rotten flesh and raw chickens?

A: They wolf them down.

■

Q: Why did the chicken cross the road?

A: He was following the player carrying seeds.

Q: Why did the player cry wolf?
A: He was looking for his dog!

■

Q: Why did the tamed cats go wild?
A: The player forgot to feed them for two days!

■

Q: Why did the player ride his horse across the road?
A: It was too heavy to carry!

■

Q: Can horses jump higher than a house in Minecraft?
A: Of course! Houses can't jump!

■

Q: What do you call a horse that neighs and whinnies?
A: A herd animal.

■

Q: What did the player say when he fell off the horse?
A: "I've fallen and can't giddyup!"

Q: **What do you call noisy horses that live in the next biome?**

A: "Neigh-bors."

■

Q: **When do Minecraft horses talk?**

A: Whinney wants to!

■

Q: **When does a sheep sound like a cheerleader?**

A: When a creeper blows him up. He goes "baaah boom baaah!"

■

Q: **How many sheep does it take to knit a sweater?**

A: None. Minecraft sheep don't knit.

■

Q: **Why do so many pigs die in Minecraft?**

A: Because there are no *h*ambulances.

■

Q: **What did the player say after he blew up the sheep?**

A: *Baaaaah boom!*

Q: What do you call a sheep with TNT?

A: A *baaaad* situation.

■

Q: Why did the cow cross the road?

A: She was following the Minecraft player carrying wheat.

■

Q: What happens if your cat dies?

A: It's a cat-astrophy!

■

Q: Did you hear the one about the cat who was an ocelot?

A: She was purr-plexed.

■

Q: Why did the cat cross several blocks?

A: To be with her player!

Q: Why did the Minecraft player love her ocelot kitten?
A: Because she was purr-fect!

■

Q: Why did the player call his dog Frost?
A: Because Frost bites!

■

Q: How do you know that all Minecraft cows are female?
A: Because all cows in Minecraft give milk.

■

Q: What do players say about Minecraft cows?
A: They should been seen and not herd!

■

Q: What do you call a coffee-colored cow that just gave birth?
A: De-*calf*enated.

Q: What type of room was the Minecraft player building for the cow?

A: A calf-ateria.

■

Q: Where was the rabbit when the lights went out?

A: In the dark.

■

Q: What type of books do Minecraft rabbits like to read?

A: Ones with jokes and hoppy endings.

■

There were two cows in a field. One mooed. The other said, "I was going to say that!"

■

Q: Why doesn't Sweden import cattle?

A: Because they have good Stockholm!

■

Q: Why did the cow cross the road?

A: He didn't want to be creamed by the player!

Q: What goes *oom oom*?
A: A cow walking backwards on a Minecraft road.

■

Q: What can you find between Pigzilla's toes?
A: Small runners.

■

Q: What does Pigzilla eat at the all-you-can-eat restaurant?
A: "Anything he wants."

■

Q: What Minecraft character is Kermit the Frog afraid of?
A: Pigzilla!

■

Q: Why should you never share your secrets with a pig?
A: Because they always squeal.

■

Q: Why can't you mix chickens with TNT?
A: They might eggs-plode.

■

If a Minecraft cow laughed, would milk come out of its nose?

Q: How do you make a Minecraft squid laugh?
A: Tickle him six times.

■

Q: In what part of Minecraft do you find a down-and-out squid?
A: On Squid Row.

■

First player: "Would you rather a giant squid attack you or a creeper?"
Second player: "I'd rather the giant squid attack the creeper."

■

Q: What famous pirate sails the open seas in Minecraft?
A: Captain Squid.

■

Q: What do you call a pig that takes up two lanes on the highway?
A: A road hog.

■

Q: What did the player say to the bat?
A: "I'm going to bat-tle you."

Q: Why did the pig jump in the water?
A: Because the player said, "Hogwash."

■

Q: Why should you be quiet around sheep?
A: Because they are ashleep!

■

Q: What do you call a sheep after a mob blows off its legs?
A: A cloud.

■

Q: What happened to the strange-colored sheep?
A: It dyed.

■

Q: How did the sheep change directions?
A: It made a ewe-turn.

■

Q: What did the pig say to the player who caught it by its tail?
A: "That's the end of me."

Q: Why did the pig cross the road?
A: Because it was the chicken's day off.

■

Q: Why do chicken coops have two doors?
A: Because if they had four, they'd be chicken sedans and we all know there are no cars in Minecraft!

■

The talented pig learned karate. Now he's dropping pork chops.

■

Q: What do you call Batman and Robin after they are trampled by Pigzilla?
A: Flatman and Ribbon.

■

Q: What happened to the pig that was struck by lightning?
A: He turned into zombie pigman!

■

Q: How did the player die from drinking milk?
A: The cow fell on him.

Q: Why did the squid cross the road?
A: To get to the other tide.

■

Q: What do you get when you pour hot lava down a rabbit hole?
A: Hot cross bunnies.

■

Q: How did the Scottish puppy feel when he saw a Wither?
A: Terrierfied.

■

Q: Why did the puppy cross the road?
A: To get to the barking lot.

■

Q: What do Minecraft players feed puppies for breakfast?
A: Pooched eggs.

■

Q: What do you call a row of rabbits that hops backwards?
A: A receding hare line.

Q: Why did the wolf cross the road?
A: He was chasing the player.

■

Q: What do you get when you cross a puppy with a calculator?
A: A dog you can count on!

■

Q: Why do Minecraft horses eat golden apples and golden carrots with their mouths open?
A: Because they have no stable manners!

■

Q: What do you call a frozen puppy in a polar biome?
A: A pupsicle!

■

Q: What did the skeleton say to the puppy?
A: "Bone appetite!"

Q: How do you turn a rabbit into toast?

A: Name him "Toast" by using a name tag or a renamed spawn egg.

■

Q: Why did the wolves cross the road?

A: The sheep were on the other side.

Q: Why did the chicken run away?

A: Because he heard the player calling fowls.

■

Knock, knock!

Who's there?

Chicken.

Chicken who?

Just chicken out your door!

■

Q: What did the player say after his sheep were blown up?

A: "Oh where, oh where, have my little sheep gone?"

TONGUE TWISTERS

Mining Minecraft Mines Make Me Merry.

Sheeps Shun Selfies.

Sheeps Say Sheariously!

Seriously Sheared Sheep.

Cows Cross Across Coarse Courses.

Colorful Cows Climb Craggy Cliffs.

Parents Protect Piglets.

Players Picked Pink Pigs.

Squash a Squirming Stepped-on Squid.

Rapid Rabid Rabbit.

Wolves Watch Witches While Witches Watch Wolves.

Chomping Chirping Chickens Chatter.

MINECRAFT LIMERICKS, POEMS, AND HAIKUS

Flying unaware
Into very hot lava.
We catch on fire.

We sleep all day long.
And if you're invisible,
We can still see you.

■

The sheep is called Jeb.
Prism colored fluffy wool.
He shimmers all night.

■

A sheep eats grass blocks,
Which turn into piles of dirt.
And their wool grows back.

■

Tamed wolves will attack
Skeletons if unprovoked.
They're wanting the bones!

■

Teleporting wolves
Visit owners far away
In twelve blocks or more.

■

When you spot a horse,
If untamed, don't saddle him.
He will flail his hooves.

■

He whinnies and neighs.
Donkeys and mules emit brays.
Tamed horses move fast.

■

Riders are thrown off.
If your horse is in water,
It's hard to remount.

■

Skeleton horses
Sound just like normal horses.
They're made up of bones.

■

Horses can be bred.
Just feed them golden apples.
Soon babies appear.

■

Want a baby mule?
Just mate a donkey and horse.
Isn't he quite cute!

■

Ocelot kittens
Found randomly are quite fast
And are hard to catch.

■

To breed a tamed cat
Give him raw fish to enjoy.
Soon you'll have kittens.

■

Growing up too fast.
Your baby cat keeps growing.
Feed him uncooked fish.

■

Tamed cats are loyal
And will follow you around.
They purr frequently.

■

We're active night.
And hang upside down on blocks.
Lava will burn us.

A black-and-white kitten named Spot
Caused trouble all day, quite a lot.
He fell down the stairs,
Scratched all of the chairs,
And loved the attention he got.

■

Covered in sacs of ink.
From head to toe, I think.
I killed a passive squid,
And this I do not kid,
I just wish the ink were pink!

Squids move up and down
Using their tentacles to push them around
As they move away from the light.
They prefer darkness more than things that are bright.
And always remain passive in town.

■

Give two cows some wheat.
They will quickly fall in love
And make baby calves.

■

Minecraft cows in a happy *moood.*
It's wheat they fancy, their favorite food.
If they eat this, tiny calves will appear
And will draw players near
As they watch the cows being wooed.

■

Rabbits hop around.
Carrots and dandelions
Are their favorites.

■

Rabbits love carrots.
To reach them, they'll jump off cliffs,
Avoiding lava.

■

Rabbits grow up fast.
After just twenty minutes,
They become adults.

■

The killer bunny
Is faster than a rabbit
And has blood red eyes.

■

Killer bunnies hop
Much like a spider—he's fast.
Careful, he will lunge.

■

Wheat seeds breed chickens.
They produce cute baby chicks
That grow up quite fast.

■

It takes just seconds
For baby chickens to grow.
Just feed them wheat seeds.

■

Want to spawn chickens?
You have a one-in-eight chance
If you throw an egg.

■

Bats sleep all day and are active at night.
If you approach, they'll take flight.
Invisible players, they can see you!
No harm, no fear, for this is true!
Flying into lava is their demise.
And you may hear their high-pitched cries!

■

A scrawny little bat named Clark
flew up from bedrock, which was dark.
He grew big wings that were scary.
They almost looked shaggy and hairy,
so his bite wasn't worse than his bark!

■

When falling from high above
A chicken flaps its wings like a dove.
This makes them immune to being smashed
As they avoid getting crashed.
So don't give a chicken a shove!

■

Players be aware:
Stay away from untamed wolves
Spawned naturally.

■

Wild wolves, with gray hair
And long drooping fluffy tails,
Harm rabbits and sheep.

■

Distinguished by their constant growling,
It doesn't sound like howling.
The wolf's tail becomes straight.
He is looking for bait.
A hostile wolf will leave you scowling.

■

Pigs act passively.
They avoid falling off cliffs.
And they eat carrots.

■

Show him a carrot.
He will always follow you.
Sometimes he will oink.

■

The giant pig means no harm.
He'd be better off on a farm.
Knocking over everything in his path.
I try really hard not to laugh.

■

There was an old wolf whose habits
Induced him to feed upon rabbits.
When he'd eaten eighteen,
He turned perfectly green
And kept on saying, "Dagnabbit!"

■

There once was a sheep with no hair.
He felt cold and oh so bare.
He was sheared down to his toes
And right up to his nose.
Alas, that poor sheep felt despair.

DID YOU KNOW...?

Did you know that squids spawn at sea level?

Do dogs in Minecraft run in circles or in squares?

Did you know that Minecraft rabbits have such good eyesight that they can see food from a farther distance than any other mob?

Did you know that the name of the "Killer Rabbit of Caerbannog" is a tribute to the rabbit in the movie *Monty Python and the Holy Grail*?

Did you know that the Killer Rabbit of Caerbannog runs faster than normal rabbits?

Did you know that "Toast" is the name of a rabbit that was added as a tribute to a player who lost his own rabbit?

Did you know that shearing a mooshroom drops five red mushrooms and turning it into a normal cow?

Did you know that to lure a pig you must put a carrot on a fishing rod?

Did you know that you can tame ocelots by giving them raw fish?

Did you know that you can tame wolves by feeding them bones?

CHAPTER 5

SNOW AND IRON GOLEMS

JOKES

Q: Did you hear about the snow golem's murder?
A: It's a cold case.

■

Q: What happened to the snow golem who got bit by a wolf?
A: He got frostbite.

■

Q: What do you get when you cross a snow golem with a zombie?
A: Frostbite.

■

Q: What do snow golems love to put on their food?
A: Chili sauce!

Q: What happened when it became so cold in the icy biome?

A: The snow golems were holding up pictures of thumbs!

■

Q: What do you call a snow golem on rollerblades?

A: A snowmobile.

■

Q: What do you call snow golems that visit the Nether?

A: Snowballs!

■

Q: Why do snow golems often look like they are dressed for Halloween?

A: Because they wear pumpkins as helmets.

■

Q: How do you make an infinite amount of snow?

A: Trap a snow golem in a 1x1 hole and dig the snow away from under his feet.

■

Q: What would a snow golem's favorite breakfast food be?

A: Frosted Flakes.

Q: Why didn't the snow golem spawn?
A: Because he was in a snow biome.

■

Q: They are not weightless in water and despite their name they can't drown. What are they?
A: Iron golems.

■

First snow golem: "Knock, knock!"
Second snow golem: "Who's there?"
First snow golem: "Snow."
Second snow golem: "Snow who?"
First snow golem: "It's *snow* laughing matter."

■

Q: What do you call a dead snow golem?
A: Water.

■

Q: What did one snow golem say to the other?
A: "Ice to meet you!"

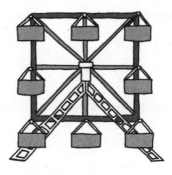

Q: Why was the iron golem sad?

A: Because the player couldn't create a round Ferris wheel.

■

Q: Why did the snow golem break up with her boyfriend?

A: Because she thought he was a flake.

■

Q: Why don't iron golems like to swim?

A: Because they rust.

■

Q: What do you get when a blaze and a snow golem meet?

A: A puddle.

Q: Why don't other mobs invite snow golems to a sauna?
A: Because they're big drips.

■

Q: What did the snow golem say to his psychiatrist?
A: "I feel abominable."

■

Q: What did the iron golem say to the player who was about to be destroyed?
A: "I'll granite you one last wish!"

■

Q: Why did everyone like the iron golem after he was struck by lightning?
A: Because he developed a magnetic personality!

■

Q: What kind of math do snow golems teach their owls?
A: Owlgebra.

■

Q: Where do snow golems keep their money?
A: In snowbanks.

Q: What happened to the snow golem that hugged a blaze?

A: He turned into a puddle of water.

■

Q: What happened to the snow golem that high-fived a blaze?

A: He melted.

■

Q: What happened to the snow golem that slapped a blaze?

A: He was destroyed.

■

Q: What do snow golems call their kids?

A: Chill-dren.

■

Q: What do you call a dead snow golem?

A: Water.

■

Q: What do you call an iron golem that does a cartwheel?

A: A ferrous wheel.

Q: What is an iron golem's favorite movie?
A: *Ferrous Bueller's Day Off.*

■

Q: If an iron golem and the silver surfer teamed up, what would you call them?
A: Alloys!

■

Q: How do snow golems make their beds?
A: With sheets of ice and blankets of snow.

■

Q: What do you call a snow golem in the desert?
A: A puddle.

■

Q: What happened to the snow golem who was stressed?
A: He had a meltdown!

■

Q: What do snow golems eat on very cold days?
A: *Sub-hero* sandwiches.

Q: What do snow golems wear on their heads?
A: Ice caps.

■

Q: What happens when two snow golems get into a fight?
A: They give each other the cold shoulder.

■

Q: Where do snow golems dance?
A: At a snowball.

■

Q: How do some snow golems travel?
A: On icicles.

■

Q: What happened to the iron golem who got bite by the snow golem?
A: He got frostbite.

■

Q: What do snow golems leave behind?
A: A trail of snow.

Q: Why did the Ender Dragon eat the iron golem?
A: Because he was anemic.

MINECRAFT LIMERICKS, POEMS, AND HAIKUS

The iron golem attacked quickly.
His victims, the mobs, were quite prickly.
They overpowered him.
He was feeling grim
Being wounded and acting quite sickly.

■

There once was a snow golem named Burt.
He wandered, got lost, and was hurt.
His figure, once svelte,
Had started to melt.
Now he's a puddle in the desert.

■

There once was a snow golem named Hannah.
She wore a bright yellow bandana.
One sunny day,
She melted away,
Because she made her way into a savanna.

■

There once was an iron golem named Bob.
His aim was perfected on mobs.
He hit each one well,
That all of them fell,
And his attackers became a big blob.

■

Patrolling the villages is their passion.
Being close to the edges of buildings is their fashion.
They don't wander far.
With villagers they will not spar.
Giving them poppies is how they show compassion.

■

Leaving trails of snow,
Snow golems carry winter
Almost everywhere.

Wanders aimlessly.
The snow golem throws snowballs
And angers the mob.

■

Passive snow golems
Drop snowballs upon their death.
Not pumpkins for you.

■

Rain, rain go away.
It's what snow golems would say,
Because rainfall hurts.

■

Place two blocks of snow
On top of one another
Then add a pumpkin.

■

With your snow body and pumpkin head,
Entering the Nether you'll soon be dead.
Throwing snowballs at angry mobs
Won't harm them or turn them into frogs.
Your best bet is to escape on a sled.

■

We're not related.
Don't hit me with a snowball.
Iron can kill snow.

■

They won't attack you unless you attack first.
It's the zombies they consider the worst.
Iron golems protect villagers from them.
It's zombies that they condemn.
So mind your own business or they will cause you to burst!

■

Avoiding lava is what iron golems do.
Lava will burn them, it's true.
Icy waters have no effect.
Yet, water they don't reject.
It's hot lava that they cannot pull through.

Don't you throw that snowball at me.
Don't chance it, for if you do, you will see.
I will get you with one quick throw.
You'll be covered in snow,
For snow golems can kill iron golems—so let it be.

DID YOU KNOW...?

Did you know that iron golems get mad if snow golems accidently hit them or hit villagers when aiming at other mobs?

Did you know that iron golems giving flowers to villager children is a reference to the ancient robots in Hayao Miyazaki's animated film *Castle in the Sky*?

Did you know that snow golems will not attack creepers?

Did you know that you need two blocks and one pumpkin to spawn a snow golem?

Did you know that snow golems can't kill slimes or magma cubes?

Did you know that villagers love iron golems because iron golems protect them?

Did you know that an iron golem needs ten doors and twenty-one houses to spawn?

Did you know that iron golems give baby villagers flowers?

Did you know that iron golems won't die if they fall—even from very high places?

Did you know that two iron golems can fight one another? They face each other, slowly back up, and then charge!

Did you know that snow golems die in the desert and in the Nether?

Did you know that snow golems are created from snow blocks and a pumpkin, and that iron golems are made from iron blocks and a pumpkin?

Did you know that if a snow golem hits a blaze with three snowballs, it will die?

CHAPTER 6
STEVE AND ALEX

JOKES

Q: What non-Minecraft character could Steve run into if he dug all the way down to bedrock?

A: Fred Flintstone.

■

Alex: "Do you know why I prefer pie to cake?"
Steve: "No, why?"
Alex: "Because pi can be squared."

■

Q: Why are Steve and Alex's puppies always being eaten in the Nether?

A: Because ghasts love hot dogs!

Q: What is Alex's favorite type of art?
A: Cubism.

Q: **What happened to Alex when she first stepped into the Nether?**

A: She was flabber-ghast-ed.

■

Q: **What did Steve say to his girlfriend?**

A: "I dig you."

■

Alex: "Did you hear that they are remodeling the floor at the daycare center?"

Steve: "Nope. What are they installing?"

Alex: "Infan-tiles!"

■

Q: **How does Steve exercise?**

A: He runs around the block.

■

Q: **What happened when Alex spawned a Wither?**

A: She didn't know *wither* to laugh or cry.

Q: How did Alex get Steve to stop texting her?
A: She blocked him.

■

Knock, knock.
Who's there?
Alex.
Alex, who?
Alex-plain later!

■

Q: What is Alex's favorite movie?
A: *How to Train Your Ender Dragon.*

■

Q: What did Alex say to the stupid zombie?
A: "I'd explain it to you, but your brain would explode."

■

Q: Why was Alex mad at the builder who told her to use a sturdier stone for her building?
A: She hates constructive criticism.

Alex: "If there were cars in Minecraft, what would the bumper stickers read?"

Steve: "I don't know. What?"

Alex: "Earth first. We'll mine other planets later."

■

Steve: "Why was the player thrilled when he found pumpkins instead of diamonds?"

Alex: "I don't know. Why?"

Steve: "Because in Minecraft, pumpkins are rarer than diamonds."

■

Steve: "How did the player hide from the creeper and the skeleton?"

Alex: "How?"

Steve: "He hid behind glass."

■

Steve: "What are a miner's three rules for finding gold?"

Alex: "I know. It's mine, mine, and mine."

Steve: "What did one PVP say to the other?"
Alex: "I don't know. What?"
Steve: "I won fair and square."

■

Steve: "Why would Picasso love Minecraft?"
Alex: "I don't know. Why?"
Steve: "Because he was a Cubist!"

■

Q: Why did Steve take a balloon ride in a thunderstorm?
A: He heard that every cloud has a silver lining.

■

Alex: "Did you know that *Annie* has a great Minecraft song?"
Steve: "No. What's it called?"
Alex: "It's a Hard-Block Life."

■

Q: What did one Steve say when he saw another Steve?
A: "Hi, Steve."

Q: What did Steve say to the other Steve when it was time to leave?

A: "Bye, Steve."

■

First player: "How does Steve chop down trees?"
Second player: "How *wood* I know?"

■

Q: Who is Steve's favorite action hero?

A: The Eggs-Terminator.

■

Q: What kind of music does Alex listen to?

A: Block and roll.

■

Q: Why did Steve have food poisoning?

A: He ate the rotting flesh from a zombie.

■

Alex: "How good is Minecraft?"
Steve: "It's top-Notch!"

Q: How does Steve pick his nose?
A: With a pickaxe.

■

Alex: "Hey, Steve, this game is too easy."
Steve: "Then step it up a Notch!"

■

Alex: "Hey, Steve, did you get the Minecraft jokes I sent you?"
Steve: "No, they're all blocked."

■

Q: What does Steve sleep on?
A: Bedrock.

■

Q: What did one Steve say to another Steve just before he killed him?
A: "Bye, Steve, bye!"

■

Q: Why is Steve so proud of his children?
A: Because they're chips off the old block.

Q: What did the Ender Dragon say when he saw Steve dressed in armor?

A: "Oh, no! Canned food."

■

Q: What did Steve say to another Steve?

A: "You're such a copycat!"

Q: How many Steves does it take to change a lightbulb?
A: None. There aren't any lightbulbs in Minecraft.

■

Q: Why did Steve cross the road?
A: To say hi to Steve.

■

Q: Why did Steve cross the road?
A: To get away from Steve.

■

Q: Why did the chicken cross the road?
A: Also to get away from Steve.

■

Q: Why couldn't Steve cross the road?
A: Because he hadn't built it yet.

■

Q: Why couldn't Steve get into the house?
A: The door was blocked.

Q: How many meals does Steve eat every day?
A: Three square.

■

Q: What did Steve say to the skeleton?
A: "I have a bone to pick with you."

■

Steve: "Did you hear about the new Minecraft movie?"
Alex: "Yes, it's a blockbuster!"

■

Alex: "You tell so many jokes!"
Steve: "It's true! And these jokes *Nether* end!"

■

Alex: "What is the national sport of Minecraft?"
Steve: "Boxing."

■

Alex: "Why couldn't the Minecraft player vote?"
Steve: "Because he was a miner."

Alex: "Why are there no carts in Minecraft?"
Steve: "Because square wheels don't roll well."

■

Alex: "Why are there no wagons in Minecraft?"
Steve: "Because square wheels don't roll well, either!"

■

Q: What's the difference between Alex and an archaeologist?
A: Alex hates finding skeletons underground.

Q: How did Steve make the player change directions?
A: He blocked her path.

■

Alex: "Why is your head shaped like a block?"
Steve: "Well, it's a long story. I was digging and came across a magic lamp. I rubbed it, and out popped a genie."
Alex: "What did you wish for?"
Steve: "See that beautiful mansion over there? I wished for that, and it appeared. Then I wished for the power to defeat the Ender Dragon. I think I messed up my third wish. I wished for a block head!"

■

First player: "Steve was so sad."
Second player: "How sad was he?"
First player: "He was so sad that he hit bedrock bottom."

■

Q: What has four legs and goes boom?
A: Two Alex's fighting over TNT.

Q: Why did Steve throw eggs at the creeper?
A: He wanted them ssscrambled.

■

Q: Why did Steve walk across the road?
A: Because there are no cars in Minecraft.

■

Q: What did the creeper say to Steve?
A: Sssurprise!

■

Q: What did the creeper say to Steve?
A: Nothing. It just blew up.

■

Q: What do you get when cross a spider with Alex?
A: Death.

■

Q: Why did Alex need homeowner's insurance?
A: Her house kept blowing up.

Q: Why does Steve like having a mooshroom as a roommate?
A: Because the mooshroom is a fungi.

■

Alex: "Why are there no cars in Minecraft?"
Steve: "Because I haven't invented the internal combustion engine yet."

■

Q: Why couldn't Steve finish writing his book?
A: He had writer's block.

■

Steve: "I'm writing this book for Minecraft players."
Alex: "Wow. Do you think people will get it?"
Steve: "Well, it's niche humor . . ."
Alex: "I would say it's *Notch* humor."

■

Steve: "Which came first, the chicken or the egg?"
Alex: "I don't know. Ask Notch."

■

Q: What did the TNT say to Steve?
A: "I'll blow you to pieces."

Q: What's Steve's favorite type of dancing?

A: Square dancing!

Steve: "How are amino acids related to Minecraft?"
Alex: "I don't know. How?"
Steve: "They're both building blocks of life."

■

Steve: "Why was the Minecraft player so good at boxing?"
Alex: "Why?"
Steve: "Because he could block a punch."

■

Q: What crime-catching skills do Minecraft police excel at?
A: Putting up road blocks.

■

Alex: "How many blocks fit in an empty chest?"
Steve: "One, because after one, it's no longer empty."

■

Q: Why doesn't Steve get invited to parties?
A: He's too square.

Q: Why does Steve have trouble solving problems?
A: He has trouble thinking outside the box.

■

Q: What is Steve's favorite party appetizer?
A: Cheese cubes.

■

Q: What does Alex do each time she slays a creeper?
A: Puts a Notch on her sword.

■

Q: Why couldn't Steve go on the Internet?
A: It was blocked.

■

Q: Why did Steve think Alex was hot?
A: She was on fire.

■

Q: Why did Alex think Steve was hot?
A: He was drowning in lava.

Q: What type of pizza does Alex like?
A: Sicilian.

■

Q: What did Steve say to his girlfriend?
A: "You stole 9.5 of my hearts!"

■

Q: What type of music can't Alex and Steve sing together?
A: A round.

■

Q: What type of floor did Alex put in the house she built for her pet snake?
A: Rep-tile.

■

Q: Why does Alex put spells on her armor?
A: It makes her an enchantress.

■

Steve: "What do you get when you cross a snake with a Minecraft builder?"
Alex: "A boa constructor."

Steve: "Why do Minecrafters build with blocks?"
Alex: "They can't build with spheres."

■

Q: Why did Steve wear rocks for shoes?
A: He thought they were cobbler-stones.

■

Q: What do you get when you cross a cave spider with Steve?
A: A dead Steve.

■

Q: What did Steve say to Alex?
A: "I dig your style."

■

Q: Why couldn't Alex answer Steve's question?
A: Her mind was blocked.

■

Alex: "What do you call a polar bear in Minecraft?"
Steve: "I don't know. What?"
Alex: "Lost, because there are no polar bears in Minecraft!"

Steve: "Can a player jump higher than a tree?"
Alex: "Of course, because trees can't jump."

■

Steve: "Knock, knock."
Alex: "Who's there?"
Steve: "Markus."
Alex: "Markus who?"
Steve: "Markus down for two tickets to Minecon."

■

Alex: "What's stopping you from moving forward?"
Steve: "My mine's blocked."

■

Q: How did Alex know what move Steve was going to make?
A: She's a *mine* reader.

■

Q: Why was Steve mad at Alex?
A; Because she took him for *granite*.

Alex: "How did the student learning Minecraft drown?"
Steve: "I don't know. How?"
Alex: "Her grades were below C-level."

■

Q: Why couldn't Steve stop reading a book about helium?
A: He was so fascinated that he couldn't put it down.

■

Q: What did Steve do with the dead iron golem?
A: Barium!

■

Q: Why didn't Alex want to hear the mountain joke?
A: Because she couldn't get over it. It was blocked.

■

Alex: "What did one square block say to the other square block?"
Steve: "I don't know. What?"
Alex: "You're pointless."

Q: Why did Steve have trouble finishing his term paper?
A: He had a mental block.

■

Alex: "How is Minecraft like soccer?"
Steve: "I don't know. How?"
Alex: "Both games last for hours, nobody scores, and millions of fans insist you just don't understand."

MINECRAFT LIMERICKS, POEMS AND HAIKUS

There once was a miner named Steve
Who was proud of all that he had achieved.
As he grew older,
His reflexes got bolder
And he decided never to leave!

■

Alex built a garden on Sunday
And caught a snake that was gray.
She tried her best to make him stay.
The snake, however, slithered away.

■

Alex constructed a zoo.
She always found something to do.
When it bored her, you know,
She walked to and fro,
Then reversed it and walked fro and to.

■

Alex likes to build.
Adding more colorful blocks,
Her world simply rocks.

■

Spawned in a new world.
Alex gathers resources.
First she collects wood.

■

A crafty good player named Steve
Would stop at nothing to deceive.
He played all night long,
Until his skills became strong,
And would stop at nothing, I believe.

■

Steve won't stop digging.
He searches in vain for jewels
And sparkling diamonds.

■

Oh no, here he goes.
Steve's falling down a tunnel.
Deeper, faster, SPLAT!

DID YOU KNOW...?

Did you know Steve originally had a goatee? It was shaved off because it looked like he was smiling all of the time!

Did you know that Alex caused controversy when she was first released partially because Mojang stated that Steve was a male and a female skin?

Did you know that there used to be a Steve, Beast Boy, Human, Rana, and Original Steve Mobs?

Did you know when Markus Persson, the creator of Minecraft, told his high school guidance counselor that he wanted to make video games, his counselor said that probably wouldn't happen?

CHAPTER 7
HEROBRINE

JOKES

Q: How does Herobrine spy on people?
A: He uses spyders.

■

Q: What did the pro Minecraft player say to Herobrine?
A: You sure ocelot of questions.

■

Q: What did Herobrine say to the ocelot?
A: Do what I tell you, ore else!

■

Q: How did Herobrine confuse a Minecraft fan?
A: He put him in a room full of empty boxes.

Q: What did Herobrine get when he pushed a music box down a mineshaft?

A: A-flat miner.

■

Q: Why was Herobrine sent to the doctor?

A: He had a virus.

Q: How did Herobrine slow down the computer?
A: He took a couple of bytes out of it.

■

Q: Why was Herobrine afraid to go to the delicatessen?
A: Because last time he went, the deli men tried to use him to make pickles.

■

Q: Why did Herobrine visit the seashore?
A: He wanted to visit Ocean Brine.

■

Q: What did Herobrine say when he looked into the mirror?
A: "Oh, no, my twin!"

■

Q: What did Herobrine do at lunchtime?
A: He took a byte out of your computer.

■

Q: Why did Herobrine keep sneezing?
A: He had a virus!

Q: How is Herobrine like a favorite Disney dog?
A: He makes your computer go goofy.

Q: Why was Herobrine in the computer?
A: Because he wanted a byte to eat.

Q: What's Herobrine's favorite snack?
A: Chips.

Q: How could you tell Herobrine was getting old?
A: He had memory loss.

Q: Did you hear the one about the bucket of salty water that saved the day?

A: Herobrine.

■

Q: Who isn't in any versions of Minecraft, yet players say they've spotted him?

A: Herobrine.

■

Q: What's another name for Herobrine?

A: A virus.

■

To err is human, and to blame it on Herobrine is even more so!

■

To err is human, but to really mess things up requires Herobrine!

MINECRAFT LIMERICKS, POEMS, AND HAIKUS

A legend by many he's called.
In the game of Minecraft he's installed.
His name is Herobrine.
He appears to live in the mine.
Oh no, now my screen has stalled.

■

The TNT exploded.
Actually, it imploded.
It missed Herobrine's face.
He wouldn't give up the chase.
I got him while I reloaded.

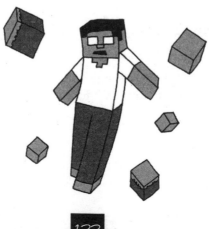

Deep into the game, Herobrine appears.
He's messing up the shaft mine gears.
I try my best to slay him.
Losing to him would be grim.
At last, I win and give three cheers.

■

As I stand on the ledge of a mine,
I create a potion to stop Herobrine.
He's causing my computer to glitch
And is making me twitch.
I vow to stop him right now.
If I only knew how.
I guess I will have to turn off the switch.

■

Is Herobrine a glitch?
He's definitely not a witch.
Some claim he's hidden inside the game.
Many others are here to proclaim.
That Notch created him as a hitch.

■

Is he a legend or is he real?
What is Herobrine's deal?
They say he's never been seen,
Though many say his shirt is green.
He looks just like Steve.
Others just don't believe.
They supposedly share the same type of skin.
Maybe they are just twins!

If you see two lights shining bright.
Beware, be quick, and take flight.
It's Herobrine coming after you.
You need a sword, one weapon or two.
You must slow him down with a brick.
On your feet, you must think quick.
TNT will do the trick!

Herobrine's a miner by trade.
You may spot him or he may fade.
He doesn't exist.
He's just a glitch.
Or your computer may need an upgrade.

■

An urban legend named Herobrine
Has a favorite pig he calls Heroswine.
He's not in the game's code.
Yet he can cause you to explode.
If you mistake him for Steve
Get out quickly and leave.

DID YOU KNOW...?

Did you know that Herobrine is said to be Notch's brother?

Did you know that Herobrine will attack any mob?

Did you know that Herobrine sometimes wears diamond armor?

Did you know that most players think Herobrine's a ghost?

Did you know that Herobrine cannot be killed?

MINECRAFT ADDICTS

You know you are addicted to Minecraft when you have fantasies of spotting Herobrine!

CHAPTER 8

WEAPONS, FLOWERS, AND JEWELS

JOKES

Q: Why did the sailor bring iron onto his ship?
A: He needed ores!

■

Q: Why don't miners mine in Oregon?
A: Because the ore is gone.

■

Q: What keeps a tree in place?
A: Square roots!

■

Q: What's red and invisible?
A: No roses!

Q: How do you prevent creepers from digging in your garden?

A: Hide their shovels.

■

Q: Why does the player prefer silver over gold?

A: Because she digs silver and pans gold.

Sticks and stones may break my bones, but now I can build a pickaxe!

■

Q: Why did Markus Persson create Minecraft?
A: He thought it would be ore-some.

■

Q: Did you hear the joke about the broken sword?
A: It's pointless.

■

Q: If a tree falls in a forest and there's nobody to see it fall, does it hit the ground?
A: The tree floats until you chop it down with an axe.

■

Q: Where do miners like to relax?
A: In a rocking chair.

■

Q: Where else do miners like to relax?
A: On bedrock.

Q: What did the player say while he continued to break rocks?

A: "Rock on!"

■

Q: What did the Minecraft pro tell the noob?

A: "May the quartz be with you."

■

Q: Why did the miner cry when his friend left?

A: He was very sedimental.

■

Q: What is The King's favorite sing-a-long song?

A: "If I Had a Hammer."

■

Q: Why did the player cross the lava?

A: Because there were twenty-nine diamonds on the other side.

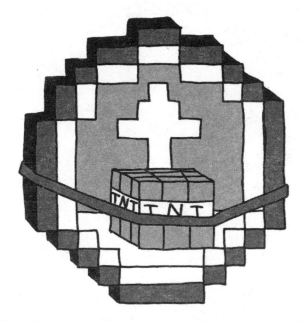

Q: What do you get if you cross a redstone clock with TNT?

A: A ticking time bomb.

■

Q: Why is a noob like an uncut diamond?

A: Both are rough around the edges and shine with some polish.

MINECRAFT LIMERICKS, POEMS, AND HAIKUS

A very smart player named Rob,
Tried to hide from a mob
By building two-block-tall flowers
That gave him hidden powers.
Oh, Rob, what a good job!

There was a young miner named Robby.
He developed a terrible hobby.
He'd knock on your door,
Drop his pickaxe on the floor,
And use TNT to blow up your new lobby.

In real life we pick them,
Removing roots and entire stem.
We don't want them in our gardens.
Yet in Minecraft we grant them pardons.
Because we know dandelions are pretty gems.

Flowers generate on dirt and grass blocks.
Dandelions and poppies grow around the rocks.
Even in biomes covered in snow,
Roses and tulips continue to grow.

■

Who ever heard of flowers blooming in snow?
We know in Minecraft it is possible though.
In a snowstorm, poppies add beautiful hues.
Despite the snow, the landscape continues to amuse.
These hardy flowers battle all elements to grow.
In the end they triumph with a decorative show.

■

There once was a player named Joel.
He mined in the dark, don't you know.
He needed light
To make things bright.
Now, Joel uses sticks and coal.

■

There once was a Minecraft player named Moe.
He searched for diamonds high and low.
They're the hardest, strongest, and rarest to find.
Despite this, he didn't mind.
Soon he saw their brilliant glow.

■

There was a young player named Max.
He wielded a giant pickaxe.
He killed a large mob
And loved doing his job
And piled them up in big stacks.

■

Chopping down a tree.
I am incredibly strong.
Using my bare hands.

■

Digging block by block,
I suddenly hit bedrock.
Searching for diamonds
And searching for gold.
Playing Minecraft never gets old.

■

With arrow in hand I take aim.
I simply love playing this game.
Watching things explode—
Buildings fall and erode.
Nothing about Minecraft is lame!

■

Roses are square.
Dandelions are square.
Tulips are square.
What do you expect?
This is Minecraft—everything is square!

■

There was an old witch.
She dug in a ditch
And found diamonds that glowed
Not too far under the road.
Now this witch is very rich!

■

Diamonds underground
Lying there just underfoot.
Beware: hot lava.

■

With a big pickaxe
I spend too much time digging
TNT's faster!

DID YOU KNOW...?

Did you know that the main flowers at Jeb's wedding were peonies?

Did you know that a Minecraft ice farm can also be used as an ordinary skating rink?

Did you know that diamond swords do the most damage?

Did you know that the wood sword does the least damage?

Did you know that in Minecraft flowers grow underground?

Did you know that not all compasses point north? In Minecraft, a compass points to the last bed you slept in!

Did you know that if you sleep in a bed, you'll skip to the next morning?

Did you know that emeralds, diamonds, gold, and redstone can only be mined with an iron pickaxe?

Did you know that emeralds can only be found in the extreme hills biome?

Did you know that the three weapons in Minecraft are lava, swords, and bows?

Did you know that swords can be made out of wood, stone, iron, gold, and diamonds?

Did you know that there are five kinds of armor in Minecraft? They are leather, gold, iron, chain, and diamonds.

Did you know that you can only get chain armor in creative mode or from a villager trade?

Did you know that roses are rarer than dandelions?

Did you know that silverfish hide in rocks and stone?

Did you know that the Ender Dragon will pass right through obsidian, end stone, and bedrock without destroying them?

Did you know that "Mojang," the name of the Swedish video game company founded by Markus Persson, is a Swedish word meaning "gadget"?

MINECRAFT ADDICTS

You know you are addicted to Minecraft when you try to plant flowers in the snow!

CHAPTER 9

ORESPAWN, MUTANT CREATURES, AND TWILIGHT FOREST MODS

JOKES

Q: What do you get when you cross Mobzilla with The King?

A: Total destruction.

■

Q: What did Mobzilla give to The King?

A: A royal pain.

■

Q: Why was the hydra put in charge?

A: Because he provides hydra-electric power.

Creeper: "How many weapons are there in the Orespawn mod?"
Zombie: "Who cares? All it takes is just one hit and you will explode."

■

Q: What's the best way to talk to a mutant creature?
A: From a distance!

Q: How do mutant zombies like their meals?
A: Runny.

■

Q: Where is a mutant creeper's favorite place to visit?
A: Lake Eerie.

■

Q: How can you tell a good mutant creeper from a bad one?
A: If he's a good mutant creeper, you will be able to talk about it later.

■

Q: Who did the mutant zombie call when he lost his head?
A: A head hunter.

■

Q: How did the mutant zombie clear his throat?
A: He spent all day gargoyling.

■

Q: On which days do mutant zombies eat?
A: Chewsday.

Q: What do single mutant zombies do at parties?

A: They go around looking for edible bachelors.

■

Q: What do you call a polite, friendly, and good-looking mutant creature?

A: A failure!

■

Q: Why do mutant creature mobs like bell-bottom pants?

A: Because they are mod!

Q: Why did the mutant zombie take his nose off?
A: He wanted to see how it runs!

■

Q: What should you do if a mutant creeper crashes through your front door?
A: Crash through your back door!

■

Q: What did the mommy mutant zombie say to her children?
A: "It's not polite to talk with someone in your mouth!"

■

First Mutant Zombie: "See that player over there?"
Second Mutant Zombie: "Yes."
First Mutant Zombie: "Well, she just rolled her eyes at me."
Second Mutant Zombie: "You should roll them back to her. She might need them!"

■

Q: What do they serve for lunch at mutant zombie school?
A: Human beans, boiled legs, pickled bunions, and eyes cream.

First Mutant Zombie: "Am I late for dinner?"
Second Mutant Zombie: "Yes, everyone's already been eaten."

■

Q: Why should you duck if a hydra sneezes?
A: He has fire breath.

Q: What did the mutant zombie vacationing on a cruise say to the ship's server at dinner time?
A: "Hold the menu, and bring me the passenger list."

■

Q: What did the blown-up mutant creeper's headstone read?
A: "Here he lies in pieces."

Q: **What did the mutant creeper say to the mutant Enderman?**
A: "Stop sucking me in!"

■

Q: **What's scarier than a normal Enderman?**
A: A mutant Enderman.

■

Q: **How is the hydra's fireball attack like TNT?**
A: It takes a few seconds before exploding when it hits the ground.

■

Q: **Why does everyone like the Twilight Forest mod?**
A: Because their habitat is filled with giant mushrooms and everyone knows mushrooms are fungis!

■

Q: **What does the Nether and Twilight Forest realm have in common?**
A: They both have glowstones that grow there naturally.

■

Q: **Who has the voice of Death?**
A: The mutant Enderman.

Q: Why were the players so hungry?

A: They were attacked by mosquito swarms.

■

Q: Why are mosquito swarms so annoying to players?

A: Because they get under their skin.

Q: What's a mutant creature mod's favorite form of art?
A: Modernism.

■

Q: Why are mosquito swarms so annoying to players?
A: Because they get under their skin.

■

Knock, knock.
Who's there?
Anna.
Anna, who?
Anna another swarm of mosquitoes.

■

Knock, knock.
Who's there?
Raven.
Raven who?
Raven lunatic player if you don't open this door!

MINECRAFT LIMERICKS, POEMS, AND HAIKUS

Exploring Twilight Forest mod is enthralling.
Perhaps it's the light from glowstones sprawling?
Discovering new creatures like rams, deer, and fireflies,
Makes this realm one that I prize
And adds a new level to my calling.

■

There once was a large Minotaur.
He's prepared to start a war.
Stay out of his line of vision,
For if he sees you, it will be his decision
To charge at you like a wild boar.

■

There once was a mutant Enderman named Bob.
He acted like such a terrible slob.
He never stayed clean
And was so terribly mean
That he angered numerous mobs!

■

DID YOU KNOW...?

Did you know that the Orespawn mod added more than 15 weapons, 100 bosses, and 60 mobs?

Did you know that if The King battled Mobzilla that there would be nothing left?

Did you know that the Orespawn mod has a ton of weapons and tools?

Did you know the Orespawn mod also has armor, mobs, and bosses?

Did you know that a mutant Enderman can carry four blocks and can also throw them at you?

Did you know that time travel slows the hydra down so it's easier to escape from him?

Did you know that mosquito swarms don't fly?

Did you know that mosquito swarms make loud buzzing sounds when you are near?

Did you know that deer living in the Overworld make the same sounds as cows?

CHAPTER 10

MINECRAFT PLAYERS

JOKES

First player: "Hey, what are you reading?"
Second player: "A review of a new Minecraft YouTube video."
First player: "What does it say?"
Second player: "It's iron-y, comedy gold, *glassic*, and will have you lava-ing in your face."

■

Q: What are Minecraft YouTubers called?
A: Blockheads!

■

Q: Why did the video game player cross the road?
A: To play Minecraft!

Q: What does a proud Minecraft dad call his son?
A: A chip off the old block.

■

First player: "Why is a fire drill not a good idea in Minecraft?"
Second player: "Why?"
First player: "Because in school we line up and act orderly. In Minccraft, when there's a fire, you need to run!"

■

Q: What do you call it when your dad beats you at Minecraft?
A: Mid-life crisis.

■

Mom of Minecraft player: "I wish there was a game on US history that's as popular as Minecraft."
Dad of Minecraft player: "Why?"
Mom of Minecraft player: "Because our son flunked his history test and he knows everything there is and more about Minecraft."

Q: **What's a Minecraft player's favorite food?**
A: *Notch-os*!

■

Q: **Why can't Minecraft players get anything done?**
A: Because they never get a round to it!

MINECRAFT LIMERICKS, POEMS, AND HAIKUS

There once was a player named Ray.
He sat down at his computer and started to play.
He clicked on Minecraft
And almost fell into a mineshaft.
And decided to play all day!

■

There once was a player named Mary.
Of hostile mobs she grew wary.
A fierce battle she won,
Defeating them was pure fun,
Even though it was quite hairy.

■

There once was a player, a kind fellow,
Who dyed sheep a very bright yellow.
Red, blue, and bright green,
All had a perfect sheen.
This fellow was also quite mellow.

■

An old ghast respawned from the past,
Entered the player's room with a blast.
He broke all the blocks,
Turning everything into tiny rocks.
He is such a pain in the gasp!

■

There once was a player named Dave.
He was known to give sheep a close shave.
He fought creepers and ghasts,
Exploding them with blasts.
Everyone said that Dave was quite brave.

DID YOU KNOW...?

Did you know that Minecraft is the most popular video game and has sold more than 42 million units?

Did you know that Minecraft has updates every single day?

Did you know that fans create new videos on YouTube about Minecraft every day?

Did you know that the only weapons skeletons use are bows and arrows?

MINECRAFT ADDICTS

You know you're addicted to Minecraft when you see a newborn baby and say, "Oh, what a cute noob!"

You know you're addicted to Minecraft when you try to get your teacher to let you do your book report on Minecraft!

You know you're addicted to Minecraft when the only time you see your parents is when you come down for dinner.

You know you're addicted to Minecraft when you put "Mastered Minecraft" on your resume.

You know you're addicted to Minecraft when you ask your doctor how many lives you have left.

You know you're addicted to Minecraft when you refuse to go outside because of the poor sound quality and shoddy graphics.

You know you're addicted to Minecraft when you name your kids Steve and Alex!

You know you're addicted to Minecraft when you get angry that real sand doesn't float.

You know you're addicted to Minecraft when you start saving up for a real diamond pickaxe.

You know you are addicted to Minecraft when you go to rock shops looking to buy redstone!

You know you're addicted to Minecraft when your mom is going on and on about something and you try to pause her.

You know you're addicted to Minecraft when you can't understand why your real wooden pickaxe won't break solid stone.

You know you're addicted to Minecraft when you think you can just gather lava and carry it back to your forge!

You know you are addicted to Minecraft when you dream in pixels!

You know you're addicted to Minecraft when you wish every day is update day!

You know you're addicted to Minecraft when you do a quick scan of every room you enter, looking for creepers.

You know you're addicted to Minecraft when someone asks you your age and you reply, "Level 14!"

You know you're addicted to Minecraft when someone asks you to tell them about the meaning of life and you say you have no idea when that version is coming out.

You know you're addicted to Minecraft when you miss two days of school and think, *that was a short game!*

You know you're addicted to Minecraft when you go outside and the sun hurts your eyes.

You know you're addicted to Minecraft when you think your fingers are in the best shape ever!

You know you're addicted to Minecraft when someone yells "Fire!" and you look for the blazes.

You know you're addicted to Minecraft when you dig a hole in your backyard looking for diamonds.

You know you're addicted to Minecraft when you don't turn off your lights at night because you think spiders will spawn!

You know you're addicted to Minecraft when you see something in the corner of your eye that's green!

You know you're addicted to Minecraft when you only eat cube-shaped foods.

You know you're addicted to Minecraft when you add an extra "s" to words with "s" in them.

You know you're addicted to Minecraft when the tea kettle whistles and you think you have a creeper in your house.

You know you're addicted to Minecraft if you think you need to drink a bucket of milk if you get bit by a spider.

You know you're addicted to Minecraft when you have nightmares about creepers and ghasts.

You know you're addicted to Minecraft if you think your cat is an ocelot and your dog is a wolf.

You know you're addicted to Minecraft when someone hisses at you and you yell, "Creeper!"

You know you're addicted to Minecraft when you draw squares instead of circles in your art class.

You know you're addicted to Minecraft when you punch a door and expect it to open.

You know you're addicted to Minecraft when you put "Builder" on your resume.

You know you've been playing Minecraft too long when you try to use sugar cubes to build your living room furniture!

You know you're addicted to Minecraft when you start each conversation talking about Minecraft.

You know you're addicted to Minecraft when you draw a square sun in art class.

You know you're addicted to Minecraft when it's no longer just a game for you!

You know you're addicted to Minecraft when you compare the real world to Minecraft at least once a day.

You know you're addicted to Minecraft when you write lists of all the mobs and mods!

AUTHOR BIOS

Michele C. Hollow is an award-winning writer who learned about Minecraft from her son, Jordon. She blogs at *Pet News and Views* and is the author of several children's books. She has absolutely no sense of humor, which her husband and son find ironic, but she doesn't get.

Jordon P. Hollow plays Minecraft every chance he gets. An avid reader, especially on the subject of Minecraft, Jordon loves mac 'n' cheese, grilled cheese, and Tastykake pies. He is a high school student.

Steven M. Hollow is an accomplished writer, actor, storyteller, puppeteer, and teaching artist. He began playing video games with the original introduction of Pong and plans to move on to other video games once he figures out how to move the paddles.